D0508884

Oxford
Better
Spelling

OXFORD
UNIVERSITY PRESS

Great Clarendon Street, Oxford, OX2 6DP, United Kingdom

Oxford University Press is a department of the University of Oxford.
It furthers the University's objective of excellence in research, scholarship,
and education by publishing worldwide. Oxford is a registered trade mark of
Oxford University Press in the UK and in certain other countries

British Library Cataloguing in Publication Data

Data available

ISBN: 978-0-19-274321-3

1 3 5 7 9 10 8 6 4 2

Printed in Great Britain

Paper used in the production of this book is a natural,
recyclable product made from wood grown in sustainable forests.
The manufacturing process conforms to the environmental
regulations of the country of origin.

With thanks to Louise John for editorial support

Oxford
OWL

For school
Discover eBooks, inspirational
resources, advice and support

For home
Helping your child's learning
with free eBooks, essential
tips and fun activities

www.oxfordowl.co.uk

Age: 7-9

Oxford
Better
Spelling

OXFORD
UNIVERSITY PRESS

Contents

Introduction

How to use this book

Better Spelling 1 has been written for children aged **7–9** to help them with their spelling. It is designed to be used to practise spellings they have already come across in their reading or learned in school.

The book is split into **3 sections**, for **7-year-olds**, **8-year-olds** and **9-year-olds**. For each age group, the words are arranged in groups of 5 for each day of the week from Monday to Friday. By following this simple **5-a-day** method, a child can learn 1000 words in 40 weeks!

Age	Number of weeks	Number of words
7	1-40	1000
8	1-40	1000
9	1-40	1000

At the end of each week, **5 words** are repeated at the bottom of the column to reinforce the spelling rules and patterns from that week.

At the end of each section, there are **3 sets** of engaging word activities to help with further practice. The **Now practise . . .** pages include themed groups of words from the words they have learned. The **Spelling help** pages reinforce common spelling rules. The **Word fun** pages contain word activities, such as solving anagrams and riddles and remembering how to spell words using mnemonics.

How are the words chosen?

The words in this book have been chosen according to the level appropriate for each age. The word groups become progressively more difficult as the child goes from **week 1** to **week 40**.

The aim of the book is to cover the variety of words and spelling patterns that a child of each age would expect to find in books, newspapers or websites suitable for that age. Additionally, it aims to build vocabulary and help children to decode more challenging words in their reading and writing. Essential words recommended for the relevant year group in the English national curriculum are also included.

Sound-based groupings help to reinforce the spelling patterns learned in the younger ages at school, linking together phonemes and graphemes that help to reinforce the different spellings. Words that children frequently misspell have been identified using the **Oxford Children's Corpus**. Further information about the **Oxford Children's Corpus** is provided at the end of this book.

The best way to learn spelling is to learn little and often. This structured **'5-a-day'** approach provides children with practical support for learning to spell not only through the years of primary school but for lifelong reading and communication skills.

Spellings
for 7-year-olds

	Week 1	**Week 2**
Monday	off sniff ill hill if	bag bat sat shall path
Tuesday	tell all dress grass bus	and land pond kind behind
Wednesday	mess buzz back trick neck	sand wand plan mad man
Thursday	bank drink thank wing song	live have give eve wave
Friday	long sing bring fill roll	legs let get mask fast

Spell it again . . .

sniff • buzz • all
drink • sing

shall • wand • behind
have • mask

Week 3	Week 4	
bed	she	**Monday**
dead	sea	
scared	key	
head	me	
end	see	
beg	ear	**Tuesday**
egg	hear	
in	here	
seven	deer	
begin	clear	
the	cheer	**Wednesday**
then	year	
tent	tear	
went	appear	
enter	tier	
wet	eat	**Thursday**
set	meet	
elf	keep	
cake	need	
basket	meat	
pen	seen	**Friday**
pencil	mean	
sent	keys	
yet	seas	
forget	sees	

scared • egg • enter
cake • forget

here • hear • appear
seas • sees

	Week 5	Week 6
Monday	feed ✓p feet speed tea leave	boat ✓p oak board oar road
Tuesday	free tree he field three	load toad snow row no
Wednesday	heel heal he'll flee we	but cut button bottom top
Thursday	peer rear near nearly beard	spoke broke hero old nose
Friday	fear ears week sweet heat	float goat glow soap goal

Spell it again . . .

leave • field • he'll
nearly • week

oar • snow • button
spoke • float

Week 7

Monday
jump
hut
hurt
turn
trunk

Tuesday
sharp
farm
dark
barn
warm

Wednesday
speak
been
cream
team
leap

Thursday
sheep
bean
each
real
idea

Friday
scream
agree
weak
beak
deal

Week 8

Monday
sneak
clean
seed
feast
peas

Tuesday
seem
treat
beach
creak
leaf

Wednesday
dream
sleep
beast
deep
teach

Thursday
meal
neat
seal
stream
leader

Friday
them
some
home
swim
come

hurt • warm • cream
each • weak

seed • feast • leader
some • home

	Week 9	**Week 10**
Monday	tail ✓ ℓ mail raise sail again	say ✓ ℓ play bay grey obey
Tuesday	lain nail paid main mane	away pay clay name race
Wednesday	lane rain fail trail male	gaze says days they ways
Thursday	grate great plane plain snake	ace age lays pays always
Friday	rat trap tap flap shape	ate plate rocket pocket ticket

Spell it again . . .

again • lain • grate
plain • shape

play • obey • ace
always • rocket

Week 11

Week 12

Monday · Tuesday · Wednesday · Thursday · Friday

Week 11	Week 12
fly	tie
buy	tip
by	lie
dry	try
cry	tried
my	ice
shy	nice
eye	rice
sigh	tyre
high	tire
time	lies
tiger	ties
hide	tied
slide	July
ride	reply
it	riding
sit	hiding
bite	eating
size	flying
site	crying
mile	dying
smile	saying
shine	going
prize	being
mime	coming

buy • eye • sigh
size • shine

ice • flying • coming
July • tried

	Week 13	Week 14
Monday	lady tiny pretty early lazy	star bar March shark alarm
Tuesday	happy scary angry angrily ready	shiny money honey monkey hungry
Wednesday	red read reed her cover	joke lucky jelly tidy buys
Thursday	after river dinner water hunter	pony story family fairy baby
Friday	palm calf maze amaze amazed	busy very berry bury every

Spell it again . . .

early • angry • angrily
water • calf

shiny • money • family
bury • every

16

Week 15

up
pop
on
upon
sun

sum
summer
sunny
tummy
funny

cage
safe
able
care
share

bear
pear
meant
leapt
crept

ache
fake
break
brake
prey

Week 16

air
fair
fare
faint
paint

hair
chair
laid
said
scare

stairs
stare
wear
there
their

bread
brain
afraid
parent
captain

earth
learn
pearl
girl
sky

Monday
Tuesday
Wednesday
Thursday
Friday

share • pear • meant
ache • prey

said • there • their
pearl • girl

	Week 17	Week 18
Monday	lick stick shock clock track	fish shop lost dig fix
Tuesday	dust burst burn heart punch	phone fat fur fog roof
Wednesday	dusty dirty crazy heavy silly	food too hook two to
Thursday	win skin inn gym myth	tooth moon do good poor
Friday	oaks thanks arms his goes	pool cool tool flood blood

Spell it again . . .

burst • heart • myth
oaks • goes

phone • fur • two
poor • flood

18

Week 19

moor
floor
or
nor
war

world
worm
wore
oars
bore

bored
closed
turned
tired
opened

horse
short
storm
order
forest

sow
so
mole
flow
though

Week 20

odd
quad
halt
salt
party

call
ball
walk
talk
small

sad
sadly
lonely
loud
loudly

before
score
know
show
slow

truck
mug
tunnel
lunch
curse

Monday
Tuesday
Wednesday
Thursday
Friday

world • wore • opened
mole • though

halt • call • lonely
before • tunnel

	Week 21	Week 22
Monday	run kerb loop wool swoop	empty bunny bully nobly simply
Tuesday	loose lose blue blew clue	bottle apple little battle giggle
Wednesday	crew drew cook grew shoot	bubble stable evil April final
Thursday	could soon would noon flew	arrive carrot worry marry hurry
Friday	redo raw roar rule arrow	muddy hairy hidden ladder cuddle

Spell it again . . .

loose • lose • would
redo • roar

empty • hurry • hairy
little • muddy

Week 23

Monday
whose
who's
group
tour
four

Tuesday
fruit
juice
build
sugar
figure

Wednesday
smell
smelly
slowly
gently
humbly

Thursday
slot
got
not
gnat
gnaw

Friday
knight
night
gnome
knew
new

Week 24

Monday
medal
meddle
middle
mumble
tickle

Tuesday
climb
lamb
him
tomb
whom

Wednesday
offer
office
are
rare
rows

Thursday
grow
fork
knock
knee
knife

Friday
actual
usual
finish
finally
puppy

who's • fruit • build
knight • gnome

medal • climb • whom
knock • finally

Week 25

Week 26

Monday

Week 25	Week 26
cheese	mist
choose	missed
chance	piece
change	peace
branch	shriek

Tuesday

desert	torch
dessert	horn
jungle	torn
handle	along
shrink	strong

Wednesday

right	normal
tide	parrot
wild	mirror
tight	matter
mild	wire

Thursday

dull	sure
dump	cure
laugh	pure
might	nature
lamp	future

Friday

taste	wasp
brick	swap
third	wrong
town	rude
snack	wrap

Spell it again . . .

dessert • right • laugh
third • town

piece • mirror • sure
swap • wrap

Week 27

oil	
foil	
coin	
boy	
joy	

enjoy
annoy
voice
noise
point

oils
buoy
toilet
join
giant

help
hole
whole
holly
brush

touch
enough
cousin
couple
trouble

Week 28

wander
wonder
farmer
woman
than

attic
awake
shake
milk
thick

window
pole
below
bone
smoke

woke
stroke
local
follow
pillow

single
during
racing
living
limiting

Monday · Tuesday · Wednesday · Thursday · Friday

foil • enjoy • buoy
cousin • trouble

attic • follow • single
during • living

	Week 29	Week 30
Monday	rabbit attack happen lesson kitten	bridge huge rage stage charge
Tuesday	letter bright invite light fight	league guard swing argue sign
Wednesday	inside decide sight beside silver	quite quick quest squeak quiz
Thursday	driver rather mother master clever	breath search really reach chest
Friday	corner doctor finger boring born	eight weigh vein rein reign

Spell it again . . .

happen • lesson • bright
decide • doctor

bridge • league • quite
eight • weigh

Week 31

Week 32

Week 31	Week 32
once	owls
since	claw
space	lawn
scene	saw
circus	sew
force	news
fence	ewe
notice	few
moth	feud
death	use
out	cute
our	fuel
house	cube
mouse	statue
cloud	radio
owl	owner
bow	alone
gown	throw
groan	crown
grown	clown
own	gone
bowl	above
brown	front
crowd	month
bawl	stole

once • scene • cloud
grown • bawl

ewe • feud • statue
above • month

25

	Week 33	**Week 34**
Monday	amber number picnic panic magic	when wheel what while white
Tuesday	pirate spider strike write kite	were where whilst whether weather
Wednesday	gather picture supper travel pebble	witch which catch watch much
Thursday	carpet present wizard almost hideous	itch pitch hatch snatch freeze
Friday	ginger danger orange jaw June	cause bows ease laws paws

Spell it again . . .

pirate • write • hideous
danger • June

whilst • whether • which
pitch • cause

Week 35

yawn	
hawk	
crawl	
sword	
answer	

growl
mouth
pound
proud
flower

sound
about
hour
power
tower

fought
around
ground
bounce
course

weird
either
friend
shield
fierce

Week 36

famous
double
you
young
tongue

jealous
obvious
curious
serious
measure

shiver
brave
alive
people
person

yolk
film
listen
half
hotel

cottage
manage
limited
lovely
nearby

Monday

Tuesday

Wednesday

Thursday

Friday

proud • fought • weird
friend • course

young • tongue • measure
people • cottage

	Week 37	Week 38
Monday	bulb box echo chorus scheme	act child angel antique science
Tuesday	effect affect except expect accept	iron human dragon ocean belong
Wednesday	action potion chef chalet machine	across prince island castle splash
Thursday	circle devil portal royal eagle	ballet shell stroll allow collect
Friday	shadow palace spring purple rescue	poem herb beautiful please prefer

Spell it again . . .

scheme • except • eagle
purple • rescue

antique • science • ocean
island • beautiful

Week 39

Week 40

Week 39	Week 40
anyway	different
maybe	asleep
cupboard	enemy
tiptoe	safely
bedroom	gloomy

disobey	nobody
anyone	mighty
illegal	planet
return	reason
refresh	defeat

mislead	yellow
misspell	jewel
snowman	wooden
myself	nasty
become	snowy

accident	puzzle
occasion	surprise
naughty	possess
museum	promise
engine	because

diary	escape
lovely	bicycle
country	mystery
happier	Egypt
tension	pyramid

cupboard • occasion
naughty • country • tension

different • surprise • because
pyramid • bicycle

Now practise...

Animal words

wasp

fly

horse

sheep

monkey

fish

rabbit

mouse

gnat

goat

hawk

shark

rat

worm

spider

bear

moth

snake

bunny

seal

puppy

kitten

tiger

owl

deer

pony

calf

mole

toad

parrot

Now practise...

Body words

finger   knee

eye   nose   head

neck   hair   heart

mouth   voice

nail   heel   ear

brain

blood   palm

back   chest   bone

tooth   beard   skin   bottom

vein   arms   legs

feet   tongue   tummy

jaw

Spelling help

Silent letters

Sometimes words have silent letters in them. Have a look at some of the words below. You have already learned to spell these words. Find the silent letter and practise spelling the words again.

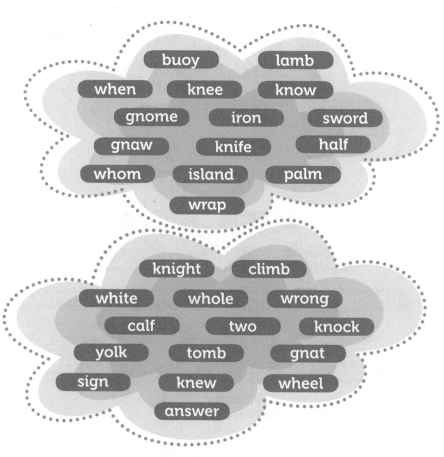

buoy · lamb · when · knee · know · gnome · iron · sword · gnaw · knife · half · whom · island · palm · wrap

knight · climb · white · whole · wrong · calf · two · knock · yolk · tomb · gnat · sign · knew · wheel · answer

Spelling help

Tricky spellings

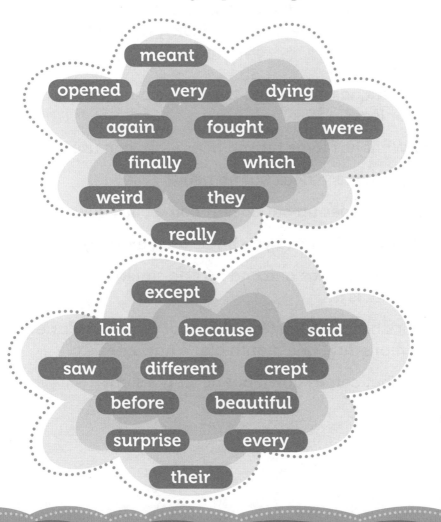

meant

opened very dying

again fought were

finally which

weird they

really

except

laid because said

saw different crept

before beautiful

surprise every

their

Based on the Oxford Children's Corpus research and analysis. See pp94–95 for more information.

Word fun

Riddles

The answers to these riddles are all words you have learned to spell. Solve the riddles. The answers are given below.

Q What has a face and two hands but no arms or legs?

Q What has to be broken before you can use it?

Q What has a neck but no head?

Q What goes up but doesn't come back down?

Q What belongs to you but is used more by others?

Q Everyone has one and no one can lose it, what is it?

Q It's been around for millions of years but it's never more than one month old. What is it?

Q What comes down but never goes up?

Answers
clock, egg, bottle, age, name, shadow, moon, rain

Word fun

More riddles

Q What five-letter word becomes shorter when you add two letters to it?

Q What is as light as a feather, but you can't hold it for more than a minute?

Q What kind of tree can you carry in your hand?

Q What hears without ears, speaks without a mouth and floats in the air?

Q What goes through towns and over hills but never moves?

Q What has a head but never cries, has a bed but never sleeps and has a bank but no money?

Q What loses its head in the morning but gets it back at night?

Q What gets broken without being held?

Spellings
for 8-year-olds

	Week 1	Week 2
Monday	game gale save lake hail	hand band stand hangs drank
Tuesday	gain tale paper pane pain	card part start started scarf
Wednesday	pale wait late train create	rich switch sick tick spin
Thursday	base stays chain contain steak	reel cheek seals sheet these
Friday	trays plays player trailer wailing	feeds weeks tease teams sweep

Spell it again . . .

hail • paper • create
contain • player

drank • started • these
tease • sweep

Week 3

spot
soft
rock
lock
shot

stop
frost
block
topic
horror

dare
declare
cared
pears
wears

ferns
herbs
shirt
stirs
earn

hold
hose
comb
moan
dough

Week 4

slip
ship
many
carry
lorry

feel
seat
easy
cheap
cheat

drip
lift
grin
wind
trip

will
cliff
class
still
spill

hate
waits
waste
waves
waved

frost • horror • declare
herbs • comb

lorry • easy • cliff
waste • waits

Monday		
	lack	foot
	duck	book
	pack	brook
	crack	shook
	check	rooks

Tuesday		
	melt	boot
	belt	boom
	dread	room
	heads	goose
	sell	hoofs

Wednesday		
	desk	peep
	test	peel
	left	beam
	well	dear
	vests	brief

Thursday		
	post	beat
	cold	teeth
	coat	eaten
	bellow	geese
	grows	niece

Friday		
	clothes	breeze
	although	screen
	croak	theme
	goals	pier
	thrown	thief

Spell it again . . .

crack • dread • grows
clothes • although

goose • hoofs • eaten
theme • thief

Week 7

Week 8

Week 7	Week 8
most	cries
over	flies
coach	fries
holes	fried
toads	tries

jokes	rise
poles	size
shows	slice
posts	timed
snows	spy

woken	slips
roses	pills
rowed	lives
shown	lived
those	winds

note	tests
hope	rests
coast	yells
blown	ebb
soaps	steps

worse	paler
worst	safer
worth	tamer
reverse	freer
surfing	icier

coach • jokes • shown
worse • reverse

cries • timed • ebb
safer • freer

	Week 9	Week 10
Monday	flat gang last snap that	steep leads seeds sixty fizzy
Tuesday	shut hunts until crumb drunk	feels kneel steam peels meets
Wednesday	judge thumb under tusks nurse	fresh smash flash shone fashion
Thursday	stung shuts jumps sucks purse	shoes finished selfish shimmer shallow
Friday	bucket rubbish thunder sudden scruffy	wish built wraps wrist wrote

Spell it again . . .

crumb • judge • jumps
sudden • bucket

kneel • fashion • finished
wrist • built

Week 11

Week 12

Week 11	Week 12	
skies	form	Monday
wakes	draws	
take	drawn	
kick	sorer	
snorkel	tall	
fore	moose	Tuesday
door	roofs	
shore	soup	
forty	tools	
lawns	ruin	
worn	move	Wednesday
forward	super	
gnaws	clues	
sort	screw	
pour	prune	
sorts	threw	Thursday
claws	through	
hawks	ruled	
thorn	look	
warns	glued	
more	full	Friday
moors	push	
straw	pulls	
hall	stood	
chalk	wound	

	Week 13	Week 14
Monday	seats means reads tears steer	bell tells cell length strength
Tuesday	hare pair fairs glare therefore	spend pretend spent bench revenge
Wednesday	earns years kerbs terms turns	stretch scratch hutch unless concern
Thursday	hears appeared hearing earring fearful	first twirl words worms work
Friday	tiers piers eerie meerkat sticker	works burns earlier service hurried

Spell it again . . .

steer • glare • therefore
appeared • tiers

strength • revenge • twirl
earlier • hurried

Week 15

bang
quack
angle
spare
compare

with
this
moths
another
neither

table
possible
pedal
petal
uncle

place
face
ancient
lace
sailing

climbed
stopped
decided
arrived
replied

Week 16

calm
army
hard
harbour
palms

called
hoard
soars
caught
warn

talks
walks
bought
walls
ought

knead
known
knelt
kneels
kneads

lakes
skier
liked
taken
kites

Monday
Tuesday
Wednesday
Thursday
Friday

angle • ancient • neither
climbed • replied

harbour • caught • bought
kneads • liked

	Week 17	**Week 18**
Monday	gazes gazed gates pages races	points buoys oiled noisy noisily
Tuesday	fewer newer feuds cures purer	split twist minute hills picks
Wednesday	newts queue stews pupil tubes	mixes mixed using onion swims
Thursday	howl round down count frown	lower nicer odder shyer wider
Friday	shout vowel flour south towel	foxes gases towns vases extra

Spell it again . . .

feuds • queue • howl
shout • flour

oiled • noisily • minute
shyer • foxes

Week 19

plant
distant
command
advance
shan't

don't
we're
we've
won't
aren't

mine
type
cried
cycle
rises

mite
wide
sighs
hire
higher

pipes
side
flight
height
hides

Week 20

you're
you've
isn't
haven't
mustn't

music
deuce
value
ewes
yew

pours
yours
thought
laundry
usually

doesn't
couldn't
wasn't
didn't
can't

none
swan
often
comment
socks

Monday
Tuesday
Wednesday
Thursday
Friday

don't • cycle • cried
flight • height

haven't • value • thought
couldn't • often

	Week 21	Week 22
Monday	cafe manor past passed gnats	bowls flown potatoes hoped soaking
Tuesday	tyres like cycling library guide	knows sparrow tomorrow suppose totally
Wednesday	lying wires sides signs tides	crews flute loses tours improve
Thursday	tying minus piles twice rides	colour concert insert opposite equal
Friday	dryer fine lightning line rhyme	they're they've mightn't wouldn't shouldn't

Spell it again . . .

cycling • guide • signs
dryer • lightning

potatoes • tomorrow
totally • opposite
mightn't

Week 23

history
victory
ability
elderly
wearily

bonfire
fighter
magnify
private
violent

sheriff
achieve
believe
barrier
experience

friends
antenna
immense
glimmer
villain

interest
serve
pattern
certain
observe

Week 24

penalty
lottery
gorilla
battery
gallery

cracked
screamed
striped
related
organised

increase
breathe
release
beneath
freedom

glisten
citizen
recent
sentence
experiment

separate
ceiling
missile
fantasy
sibling

Monday
Tuesday
Wednesday
Thursday
Friday

history • believe • friends
pattern • certain

organised • breathe
experiment • separate
ceiling

	Week 25	Week 26
Monday	poster boulder soldier builder calendar	bomb complete company comfort compete
Tuesday	ruder rarer smother stammer slipper	continue peculiar popular uniform student
Wednesday	centre glitter shatter chatter metre	funeral produce perfume execute nuclear
Thursday	capsule glimpse nostril destiny elastic	liberty February reality prickly definitely
Friday	cricket hammock unique paddock pacific	beginning receive vanilla selling extinct

Spell it again . . .

boulder • soldier • metre
capsule • unique

continue • February
beginning • definitely
receive

Week 27

snuggle
twinkle
grumble
chuckle
wriggle

miracle
dribble
shuffle
vehicle
capital

shuttle
central
wrinkle
arrival
grapple

visible
snuffle
toddler
athlete
leaflet

quay
conquer
inquire
banquet
request

Week 28

engrave
faintly
stadium
grazing
patient

willing
peeling
packing
beating
sobbing

gushing
meaning
teasing
glaring
setting

chips
chews
charity
chocolate
chamber

actually
century
chimney
natural
immature

---

vehicle • wrinkle • athlete
conquer • request

faintly • patient • chocolate
actually • immature

	Week 29	Week 30
Monday	whisper wedding wishing wounded suede	difficult saffron cough rough tough
Tuesday	important ordinary tornado fortune awkward	rampage college average fragile edge
Wednesday	orchard exhaust emerald several roaring	balloon scooter rooster cartoon shampoo
Thursday	regular consider particular remember grammar	football woods bullying cushion crooked
Friday	slither similar panther creeper warrior	howling crowded flowery astound shower

Spell it again . . .

whisper • grammar • awkward
creeper • warrior

difficult • tough • average
cushion • crowded

Week 31

Monday
eighth
weight
neighbour
beige
preys

Tuesday
weapon
feather
steady
healthy
heavily

Wednesday
dreaded
peasant
wealth
business
women

Thursday
edges
page
hedge
knowledge
passage

Friday
strange
bandage
arrange
cabbage
package

Week 32

Monday
gardener
beginner
forgetting
digging
wrapper

Tuesday
humming
swimmer
preferred
forgotten
happened

Wednesday
grabbed
covered
stepped
remembered
powered

Thursday
answered
surprised
nursery
disturb
deserve

Friday
purpose
exercise
iceberg
serpent
perhaps

neighbour • peasant
knowledge • business
strange

beginner • preferred • answered
surprised • exercise

53

	Week 33	Week 34
Monday	division invasion session version possession	gymnast typical journal court courage
Tuesday	confusion television decision collision expansion	accidental dramatic completely dramatically merrily
Wednesday	pressure treasure creature enclosure vulture	tightly ghastly basically tastefully shakily
Thursday	pleasure adventure furniture mixture feature	hastily frantically weirdly absolutely roughly
Friday	heroine vinegar medicine imagine routine	probably eagerly awfully comically quickly

Spell it again . . .

possession • treasure
adventure • imagine
routine

courage • accidental
weirdly • frantically
quickly

Week 35

gardening
startle
arguing
guarded
harmony

bizarre
garbage
harness
lasagne
frozen

husband
octopus
custard
succeed
cutting

lettuce
success
rummage
flushed
utterly

address
balance
attempt
attract
culprit

Week 36

imperfect
reappear
irregular
irrelevant
redecorate

incorrect
interrelated
supermarket
discover
disagree

international
inactive
interact
disappear
disappoint

misbehave
disease
impatient
impossible
illegible

disappeared
immortal
irresponsible
anticlockwise
autograph

arguing • lasagne • succeed
address • attempt

irrelevant • international
disappeared • impatient
irresponsible

55

	Week 37	Week 38
Monday	submarine submerge intercity superman antiseptic	magician station permission emotion discussion
Tuesday	subdivide subheading superstar biography autobiography	musician position completion injection expression
Wednesday	school character chemist chaos choir	politician mention admission invention extension
Thursday	brochure stomach chute collide provide	electrician mathematician confession question competition
Friday	scent fascinate crescent discipline descend	describe impress comprehension admiration hesitation

Spell it again . . .

school • chemist • brochure
scent • fascinate

discussion • politician
question • describe
mathematician

Week 39

Monday
sensation
preparation
information
adoration
limitation

Tuesday
nervous
vicious
dangerous
poisonous
outrageous

Wednesday
various
furious
glamorous
courageous
tremendous

Thursday
enormous
anxious
humorous
vigorous
mountain

Friday
quarter
material
diamond
extreme
extremely

Week 40

Monday
pharaoh
yacht
excitement
leopard
horizon

Tuesday
bathroom
whatever
homework
waterfall
somewhere

Wednesday
something
nowhere
someone
teenage
eyebrow

Thursday
padlock
seagull
handful
everyone
retreat

Friday
favourite
reptile
practising
develop
spontaneous

diamond • tremendous
anxious • courageous
extremely

pharaoh • somewhere
favourite • practising
spontaneous

Now practise...

Maths words

size

wide

twice

table

several

mathematician

increase

more

count

edge

weight

balance

opposite

division

height

metre

forty

angle

eighth

anticlockwise

lower

minus

quarter

length

centre

value

equal

fewer

subdivide

Now practise...

Food words

stirs   crumb

herbs   peels   chips

chocolate   custard   slice

seeds   steak   lettuce

onion   dough   saffron

flour

melt   vinegar

lasagne   healthy   pears

cabbage   stews   knead

fried   vanilla   duck

steam   cafe   fizzy

potatoes

Spelling help

Prefixes and suffixes

A **prefix** is a group of letters that is added to the **beginning** of a root word to make a new word.

A **suffix** is a group of letters that is added to the **end** of a root word to make a new word.

Here are some words with prefixes and suffixes that you have already learned to spell in this book. Look at the root words and spot the prefixes and suffixes that have been added, then practise spelling them again.

irregular   noisily
handful   eagerly   reappear
anticlockwise   impossible   quickly
submerge   incorrect   redecorate
fewer   international   illegible
impatient

submarine   misbehave
comically   disagree   irresponsible
autobiography   superman   television
immortal   excitement   immature
completely   imperfect   totally
disappeared

Spelling help

Tricky spellings

didn't

practising   wasn't   couldn't

nowhere   definitely   probably

niece   caught   business

until   tomorrow

replied

doesn't

friends   appeared   excitement

extremely   beginning   thought

arrived   through

absolutely   completely

chocolate

Word fun

Who am I?

These anagrams are made from the names of animals you have learned to spell in this book. Solve the clues and unscramble the letters.

1. GLSAELU: I am a noisy bird that lives by the seaside. I like to steal the food that you drop on the floor.

2. POTCUSO: I am a sea creature and I have eight tentacles.

3. TRENPHA: I am a wild big cat. My coat is black and shiny.

4. PLORDAE: I am also a big cat. My coat is spotted.

5. XSFEO: We like to prowl in gardens and root in your dustbins at night. We have pointed ears and bushy tails.

6. MKAEETR: I am a small furry African animal and I live with my family close around me. I stand up on my back legs and keep a lookout to guard the rest of the group.

7. SGOEO: I am a large water bird. I have webbed feet and like to honk noisily.

8. EPRSETN: I am another word for a snake.

9. VLUTREU: I am a large bird of prey that swoops down and eats dead animals.

10. TSROORE: I am a male chicken and am sometimes called a cock. I wake people up at dawn.

Word fun

What job do I do?

These anagrams are made from words you have learned to spell in this book. Solve the clues and unscramble the letters.

1. GAMICNAI: I perform tricks. Sometime I have a wand and a top hat.

2. RENREGDA: I work outdoors and I like to grow things. I can mow your lawn and look after your plants.

3. DLOSREI: I wear a uniform and I serve my country in the army.

4. RBULIED: I am a construction worker. I use bricks and other materials to put up houses.

5. CINALECERTI: My job is to fit and repair electrical equipment.

6. USCMIANI: I compose and play music.

7. YMNGSTA: I am an expert in exercises and movements that show the body's agility. I perform tumbles and somersaults.

8. SITHCME: I am an expert in chemistry. I also make and sell medicines.

9. LIOPCTINAI: I am involved in politics and help with the governing of a country.

10. ALHTTEE: I am good at physical exercises and sports, such as running and jumping. You might see me at the Olympics.

Answers
1. magician 2. gardener 3. soldier 4. builder 5. electrician 6. musician 7. gymnast 8. chemist 9. politician 10. athlete

Spellings
for 9-year-olds

	Week 1	**Week 2**
Monday	plank blank ban blanket cannot	mango tangle firing among longing
Tuesday	laps clap data nanny plait	kit tin trio robin ferry
Wednesday	cobra zebra agony tiara koala	habit rugby study fancy toxic
Thursday	saint ape tame sale painful	fry sty fright wildly stripy
Friday	behave railing slave drake mermaid	kindly slight virus tonight blindly

Spell it again . . .

blanket • plait • agony
painful • behave

trio • firing • stripy
fright • blindly

Week 3

Monday
judo
ninja
juicy
genie
major

Tuesday
garage
genius
joyful
tragic
nudge

Wednesday
dingy
trudge
emerge
jaguar
jasmine

Thursday
chief
chick
bunch
peach
fetch

Friday
chore
clutch
lurch
itchy
choke

Week 4

Monday
grape
radar
female
safety
grenade

Tuesday
bakery
parade
grace
graze
terrain

Wednesday
failure
greatly
blame
razor
blaze

Thursday
exclaim
mayor
layer
detail
waiting

Friday
sailor
explain
against
lead
led

juicy • trudge • emerge
chief • clutch

grenade • terrain • failure
mayor • against

	Week 5	**Week 6**
Monday	wine wane whirl west wheat	cub gum pluck furry supreme
Tuesday	towards whisk waist showers reward	dot plotted hundred heard herd
Wednesday	penguin wary weary wail whale	cob golf robber robbery blurry
Thursday	swans swamp swish swarm sweaty	art prank slap slam crinkle
Friday	sweetly suite require squid squishy	filthy ninth thirty sixth thrill

Spell it again . . .

whirl • towards • whale
suite • require

supreme • plotted
blurry • thirty • heard

Week 7

Monday
bath
bathing
farther
further
father

Tuesday
flea
plead
cheeky
lever
screech

Wednesday
heave
reveal
coffee
donkey
evening

Thursday
creaky
repeat
sneeze
meteor
freezer

Friday
indeed
speech
scenery
relief
relieve

Week 8

Monday
loads
loaded
loading
excited
excitedly

Tuesday
closely
enclose
crumble
crumbly
rumble

Wednesday
between
fifteen
sixteen
canteen
sardine

Thursday
bike
vine
diet
twenty
plenty

Friday
grant
enchant
panting
servant
serving

---

farther • screech • coffee
evening • relieve

excitedly • crumbly
sardine • twenty • diet

	Week 9	**Week 10**
Monday	cove stake rocky checked parking	tribe spiral primary buying satisfy
Tuesday	wreck smirk murky chaotic lilac	nicely advice advise adviser advisor
Wednesday	bulky husky sticky cracker crackle	remove removal remain remains rejoice
Thursday	litter theatre clatter motor creator	mobile stride polite realise recognise
Friday	admire inspire terrier carrier blister	capsize stripe survive precise despise

Spell it again . . .

wreck • chaotic • theatre
inspire • creator

spiral • buying • despise
rejoice • polite

Week 11

quiet
treacle
trickle
knuckle
freckle

hurtle
gentle
turtle
total
beetle

squeal
equally
squad
square
squawk

liquid
squirt
quietly
quiver
squidgy

squeeze
qualify
quality
squelch
squeaky

Week 12

scuttle
title
settle
digital
skittle

Martian
martial
trial
serial
cereal

musical
article
cubicle
medical
cackle

tackle
rustle
bustle
whistle
wrestle

drizzle
shovel
marsh
tissue
species

Monday

Tuesday

Wednesday

Thursday

Friday

quietly • equally • treacle
gentle • total

digital • cereal • whistle
tissue • species

	Week 13	**Week 14**
Monday	puddle candle waddle riddle paddle	polo awoke video meadow poacher
Tuesday	bundle bridal bridle gobble wobble	solar remote hollow propose swallow
Wednesday	rubble marble stumble tremble bramble	episode fellow toast throne hopeful
Thursday	capture venture gesture lecture conjure	borrow trophy explode promote grocery
Friday	cocoa throat narrow solo globe	bullet torrent cookie pudding igloo

Spell it again . . .

bridal • tremble • gesture
narrow • throat

meadow • episode • trophy
torrent • cookie

Week 15

tsunami
ghoul
spooky
cruel
route

scuba
surely
include
raccoon
coop

canoe
pollute
cruise
recruit
sewer

sprout
outfit
aloud
allowed
voucher

crouch
bouncy
powder
soundly
brownie

Week 16

screams
screaming
reserve
crystal
syringe

mare
airport
despair
barely
scarily

evacuee
rescuer
tulip
stupid
refuse

excuse
duvet
studio
useful
confuse

consume
costume
formula
amusing
presume

Monday
Tuesday
Wednesday
Thursday
Friday

tsunami • cruise • brownie
crouch • allowed

syringe • scarily • evacuee
amusing • rescuer

	Week 17	**Week 18**
Monday	colours odour journey fourth source	guards gallop guilty brigade dagger
Tuesday	council scowl proudly however drought	burger galaxy underground goddess ragged
Wednesday	plunge sledge badger sponge magical	guessed guest stagger snigger trigger
Thursday	general legend fridge object soldiers	starve market parcel barrel married
Friday	dustbin postman upright upgrade gateway	barking smartly passing leotard chariot

Spell it again . . .

journey • scowl • however
badger • soldiers

guards • guilty • married
starve • galaxy

Week 19

himself
herself
without
forever
itself

tomato
karate
massage
collage
piranha

glowing
diving
string
walking
amazing

talking
sitting
feeling
reading
dancing

working
singing
writing
calling
shaking

Week 20

polar
roller
burglar
collar
author

emperor
loser
proper
canter
hamster

chapter
temper
shelter
officer
clutter

suffer
murmur
drummer
rubber
locker

monitor
tractor
foster
altar
alter

Monday
Tuesday
Wednesday
Thursday
Friday

herself • without • massage
talking • writing

author • officer • murmur
tractor • burglar

	Week 21	Week 22
Monday	glory dwarf orphan drawer drawing	restore storage sorting torment divorce
Tuesday	porch scrawny pause stall aboard	vault fault explore applaud already
Wednesday	saunter salty mould sauce saucer	assault snoring royalty sore soar
Thursday	stalk launch stormy ordered haunted	install perform shortly torpedo forth
Friday	autumn record afford morning mourning	sadness endless confess suppress cutlass

Spell it again . . .

drawer • aboard • saucer
autumn • mourning

vault • applaud • suppress
explore • install

Week 23

sniffle
freaky
coffin
draft
draught

dolphin
griffin
effort
defend
defence

offence
shifter
phantom
muffle
perfectly

fluster
raffle
triumph
flicker
buffalo

lumps
chomp
clump
temple
trample

Week 24

grumpy
simple
camping
cramped
crumple

example
vampire
whimper
compliment
complement

spa
spark
sparkle
sparkly
fully

crunch
scrunch
crunchy
terror
terrify

dye
tyrant
syrup
petrify
anxiety

Monday
Tuesday
Wednesday
Thursday
Friday

draught • defence • phantom
triumph • freaky

dye • terror • complement
sparkly • anxiety

	Week 25	Week 26
Monday	lantern prevent seventy radiant pendant	tread expel examine regret instead
Tuesday	con blonde beyond respond diamonds	ebony spread arrest petrol heading
Wednesday	remind slender meander suspend blender	twelve packet honest leather dense
Thursday	worried spotted pointed warmth warming	velvet kennel strait straight trench
Friday	wicked vivid beloved ashamed skilled	nerve curry thirsty cutlery surgery

Spell it again . . .

radiant • diamonds • worried
beloved • meander

examine • arrest • twelve
straight • surgery

Week 27

Monday	energy scurry mercy circuit eternal
Tuesday	alley neigh sleigh trolley holiday
Wednesday	manner worship cancer luxury whispered
Thursday	memory factory bravery stationary stationery
Friday	violet wicket biscuit coconut racket

Week 28

Monday	poppy lolly sonic scroll brother
Tuesday	predict deflect product practice practise
Wednesday	strict protect contact suspect reflect
Thursday	attach twitch clench butcher channel
Friday	catcher ostrich choice loyal destroy

energy • circuit • neigh
luxury • biscuit

brother • butcher • ostrich
choice • destroy

	Week 29	**Week 30**
Monday	siren demon dozen melon raven	vision mission mansion passion section
Tuesday	broken prison crimson eleven cannon	auction fiction random kingdom boredom
Wednesday	beckon summon season kitchen dungeon	firmly scaly slyly hardly softly
Thursday	opinion galleon minion million billion	deadly easily neatly wrinkly funnily
Friday	tighten flatten quicken blacken swollen	calmly nastily harshly vaguely mostly

Spell it again . . .

dozen • prison • galleon
kitchen • tighten

vision • auction • wrinkly
vaguely • easily

Week 31

signal
signing
ignore
design
gnarled

dummy
skinny
beauty
gravity
balcony

cuddly
exact
crossly
briskly
briefly

knowing
turning
hanging
driving
washing

helping
killing
banging
keeping
moaning

Week 32

begging
tapping
rapping
winning
winner

ironing
aisle
isle
silent
silence

streak
ticking
striker
knocker
tracker

spirit
isolate
inherit
idiot
idiotic

scatter
spanner
cluster
scrape
scraper

Monday
Tuesday
Wednesday
Thursday
Friday

design • gnarled • beauty
briefly • knowing

ironing • aisle • knocker
isolate • spanner

	Week 33	Week 34
Monday	deliver cleaner flipper crusher invader	ascent descent assent dissent accent
Tuesday	peckish stylish babyish camera dilemma	proceed precede process actor actress
Wednesday	devious ominous tedious control pistol	recycle replace untie unlike display
Thursday	horrid horrify lighter delight lightly	unable unfair unusual unscrew uncover
Friday	prophecy prophesy prophet profit profile	dismiss unleash unravel remark convert

Spell it again . . .

stylish • dilemma • devious
delight • prophecy

ascent • precede • recycle
unusual • unleash

Week 35

unite
reunite
united
unlucky
luckily

spear
sneer
nearer
tearful
bearded

dropped
cursed
spoilt
smashed
whacked

involve
shrivel
approve
envelop
captive

leaning
weeping
dashing
healing
heating

Week 36

lunge
sausage
javelin
tragedy
apology

vintage
agitate
justice
agility
jogging

pulse
glance
massive
intense
embrace

grimace
terrace
conceal
device
devise

insist
principal
principle
licence
license

reunite • dropped • spoilt
envelop • weeping

sausage • agitate • conceal
devise • license

	Week 37	**Week 38**
Monday	seize zombie result lizard resist	babysit archway anymore keyhole goodbye
Tuesday	clumsy criticise puzzled buzzing crazily	harvest carcass archery charger bombard
Wednesday	victim problem welcome venom tantrum	gadget luggage majesty splodge hostage
Thursday	stutter plastic cascade mustard slumber	sawdust highway haircut manhole halfway
Friday	plaster smuggle scanner steal steel	hallway bedside firefly popcorn bagpipe

Spell it again . . .

seize • zombie • clumsy
cascade • smuggle

goodbye • gadget • luggage
firefly • archery

Week 39

mankind
cockpit
lookout
output
outdoor

fulfil
unicorn
nothing
shudder
lobster

mammoth
whisker
shadowy
exhibit
clamber

jubilee
beastly
thankfully
cunning
thermal

volcano
cabinet
plummet
robotic
academy

Week 40

samurai
guinea
suicide
termite
destine

lioness
cashier
pursuit
lunatic
satchel

gazelle
console
auntie
climax
furnace

trident
acrobat
vibrant
spindly
arena

replica
gremlin
titanic
trapeze
grizzly

outdoor • whisker • beastly
cunning • plummet

samurai • gazelle • pursuit
auntie • trapeze

Now practise...

Science words

volcano

explode scanner thermal

record toxic spiral result

tissue surgery odour recycle

safety pollute circuit

syringe species virus

polar

examine data

explore globe liquid

nerve galaxy meteor powder

formula energy radar

solar crystal spark

gravity

Now practise...

Sports words

qualify   canoe

scuba   trophy   walking

jogging   arena   golf

judo   tackle   dancing

karate   offence   locker

javelin

practise   trapeze

winner   rugby   energy

archery   agility   diving

pulse   martial   gallop   wrestle

leotard   polo   applaud

striker   defence   laps

acrobat

Spelling help

Homophones

Homophones are words that sound the same, but have different meanings and spellings from one another. It is easy to confuse homophones. Here are some homophones you have already learned to spell. Have another look at them and be careful not to get them mixed up!

wail – The baby let out a wail.
whale – The killer whale swam in the sea.

heard – I heard what you just said!
herd – In the distance I saw a herd of elephants.

aloud – The teacher read the story aloud.
allowed – We are not allowed to eat too many sweets.

draft – I wrote a draft of the story before I wrote the real thing.
draught – There's a cold draught coming in through the door!

-ise or -ize?

Most words ending in **-ise** or **-ize** can be spelled either way in English in the UK. You might see any of these words spelled with an **-ize** or **-ise** ending.

realise / realize   recognise / recognize
organise / organize   criticise / criticize

However some words can only be spelled with an **-ise** ending. These words are:

advise   despise   exercise   surprise   anticlockwise

Spelling help

Tricky spellings

heard

whacked   gnarled   autumn

excitedly   creaky   blurry

luckily   colours   burglar

diamonds   guards

despair

instead

soldiers   writing   screaming

quietly   allowed   straight

already   worried

relief   between

against

Based on the Oxford Children's Corpus research
and analysis. See pp94–95 for more information.

Word fun

Mnemonics

Mnemonics are phrases or rhymes that can help you to remember the spelling of tricky words. You can make up your own mnemonics – sometimes the sillier they are, the easier they are to remember! Here are mnemonics for some of the words you have just learned in the last section of this book.

autumn
An ugly troll upset my nana!

heard / herd
You h**ear** with your **ear** and a herd is a group of cattle!

Whenever there is a Q, there is a U too!

require	quality	squelch	quietly
quicken	squidgy	squeaky	equally

practice / practise
The word **ice** is a noun so prac**tice** is also a noun.
Practise is a verb.

Football practice improves your skills, so you need to practise regularly.

stationery / stationary
stationery contains **er** and so does pap**er**.
stationary (not moving) contains ar and so does car.

principal / principle
Your princi**pal** can be your **pal**.

complement / compliment
Compl**e**ment adds something to make it **e**nough.
A compl**ime**nt puts you in the **lime**light.

Word fun

Words in words

Sometimes you can find small words inside big words.
Find the smaller words in these words and practise spelling
them again.

mustard   cleaner

however   mermaid   meander   against

tracker   camera   behave   terrace

reward   blender   massage   heard

worship   terrain   stripy

whispered

odour   screams

bagpipe   allowed   upright   badger

bramble   proper   narrow   theatre

enchant   explode   despair

million   smuggle   wrestle

cereal

Useful information

The Oxford Children's Corpus

The word 'corpus' means 'a large body of words'. The **Oxford Children's Corpus** is a large electronic database which contains over two hundred million words from language written for and by children aged 4 to 14 years. The **Oxford Children's Corpus** is a unique and growing resource that helps children's dictionaries reflect the language that children encounter in their reading and writing, through books and websites.

Software tools are used to analyse this resource to give insights into the way children read and use language. It helps to identify new words and meanings coming into the language, common issues with grammar and punctuation and also the words that children find tricky to spell.

Based on contemporary children's language analysis, **Oxford children's dictionaries** are able to provide support for all these different types of spellings that children need help with.

Oxford dictionaries for children are contemporary, authoritative, engaging and age appropriate. They include first word books, dictionaries, thesauruses and digital resources to support children through school.

These dictionaries are compiled by lexicographers and backed by educational consultants, teachers, curriculum specialists and the **Oxford Children's Corpus**.

With the help of the **Oxford Children's Corpus** the **Oxford dictionaries** team is able to create the most up-to-date word and language reference tools to help children become the best communicators in life and develop a lasting love for words and language.

Also available:

Age 7+

Age 7+

Flash cards

Age 7+

Age 7+

Age 8+

Age 8+

Age 10+

Age 10+

For more vocabulary and skills practice:

Age 8–9

Age 9–10

Age 10–11⁺

Age 10–11⁺ stretch